T5-AFU-533

101 FLOWER ARRANGEMENTS
STYLISH HOME IDEAS

Hylas Publishing
Publisher: Sean Moore
Cretive Director: Karen Prince
Designer: Gus Yoo
Editor: Beth Adelman

First Published in 2003 by
BBC Worldwide Ltd,
Woodlands, 80 Wood Lane, London W12 0TT
All photographs © BBC *Good Homes* magazine
2003 with the following exceptions: pages 33,
35, 65, 89, 91, 93, 95, 97, 133 and 157 © *BBC
Homes & Antiques* magazine 2003; pages 37, 39,
41, 43, 45, 67, 69, 71, 73, 75, 77, 99, 101, 159,
197, 199, 201, 203, 205, 207 and 209 supplied
courtesy of The Plants and Flowers
Association.

Published in the United States by
Hylas Publishing
129 Main Street, Irvington,
New York 10533

Copyright © BBC Worldwide 2003

The moral right of the author has been asserted.

ISBN 1-59258-029-7

Edited by Alison Willmott
Commissioning Editor: Vivien Bowler
Project Editor: Julia Charles
Series Design: Claire Wood
Book Design: Kathryn Gammon
Design Manager: Annette Peppis
Production Controller: Christopher Tinker

First American Edition published in 2003
02 03 04 05 10 9 8 7 6 5 4 3 2 1

All rights reserved under International and
pan-American Copyright Conventions. No part
of this publication may be reproduced, stored in
a retrieval system, or transmitted in any form or
by any means, electronic, mechanical, photo-
copying, recording or otherwise, without the
prior written permission of the copyright owner.

Set in Amasis MT and ITC Officina Sans

Printed and bound in the UK by Butler and
Tanner, Ltd.
Color origination by Radstock Reproductions
Ltd, Midsomer Norton

Distributed by St. Martin's Press

101 FLOWER ARRANGEMENTS
STYLISH HOME IDEAS

Julie Savill

HYLAS
PUBLISHING

BBC

CONTENTS

INTRODUCTION

There's no denying that flowers do something quite magical to a room. Add a few blooms to a space that looks lifeless and suddenly the mood lightens, colors look fresh and you can't help but feel more relaxed and at home.

One thing we should all do is stop considering flowers as an infrequent luxury only to be enjoyed on special occasions. It's lovely to be given flowers as a gift, but it's even nicer to indulge yourself on a regular basis. And if you buy what's in season and plentiful, there's no reason why it should be an expensive extravagance. Corner florists offer an affordable and convenient way to buy flowers with your weekly shopping, and even supermarkets have improved the choice and quality of their flowers, so all you need is a few clever ways to display

them to make an instant difference in your home.

101 Flower Arrangements isn't a flower arranging book in the traditional sense, but more of a sourcebook of ideas and information to get you thinking about what is possible. Of course, all the ideas here are meant to be copied, but they are also meant to be adapted and improved upon to suit you and your home. So if you see an idea you like using carnations but you prefer gerbera, go ahead, swap the flowers and create something new and individual.

Modern flower arranging relies far more on chic, casual displays than on massed formal bouquets, so a few flowers can go a long, long way. One of *BBC Good Homes* magazine's regular contributors, and someone who deserves special thanks for all her ideas, is the hugely talented Jane Packer, who manages to capture the mood of the moment with a simplicity that you just know you can copy for yourself at home. Many of her projects are featured in *101 Flower Arrangements* and they really do prove that with the right inspiration any of us can create stylish flower arrangements in a matter of minutes.

The blissful thing about today's attitude toward flowers is that there are no real rules and no special equipment required. With a little lateral thinking ,almost anything that will hold water—from an old tin can to a teapot—can be pressed into use as a vase. Florist Jane Hughes has a real flair for flowers and unusual ways to use them ,and deserves our thanks for the witty, creative ideas you'll find in this book.

At *BBC Good Homes* magazine we have worked with some of the very best florists, and we would like to thank Nick Green who was the very first florist to contribute to the magazine, Marcus Crane for his beautiful and romantic arrangements, and The Plants and Flowers Association for all their ideas and support.

Julie Savill, Editor
BBC Good Homes magazine

Peas plus

Use your imagination and combine flowers with other natural materials to give a simple display an individual look. Vegetables offer an irresistible selection of colors, shapes and textures, and ordinary, everyday ones can look just as effective as the more exotic varieties. This display teams sweet peas with their edible namesakes, with the bright green of the peas making a striking contrast to the delicate pinks and mauves of the petals. Arrange the flowers in a clear glass vase, pack in the peas so that they hide the stems, then add water.

TIP
Although sweet peas are short-lived as cut flowers, they are easy to grow from seeds, so if you have a garden it could provide a constant supply during the summer months.

Shades of green

If brightly colored blooms are a bit too brash for your taste, an all-green arrangement makes a serene and sophisticated alternative. Foliage or green-tinted flowers with sculptural shapes make an elegant statement against a cool, contemporary backdrop. To add interest, mix different textures and shades of green, combining fresh limes with darker emeralds, as in this display. Standing tall in a clear glass vase, calla lilies, spiky papyrus and glossy Swiss cheese plant leaves strike a powerful pose. The vase tapers toward the neck, holding the tall stems firmly in position.

Fruit cocktail

As well as being a feast for the eyes, this exuberant
mix of colorful citrus fruit and gerbera blossoms is a
scent sensation; it has a refreshing fragrance that's pure
summer. Simply fill a shallow glass bowl with water,
then slice oranges, lemons and limes in half and float
them cut side up. Intersperse the fruits with mini gerbera
blossoms in yellow, pink and red, then add a few sprigs
of mint for extra scent. This would make a wonderfully
aromatic table centerpiece for a summer meal.

Berry tasty

Floating arrangements in shallow glass bowls are
strong candidates for use as table centerpieces, and
look particularly delicious when they include some juicy
fruits. Soft fruits don't deteriorate very quickly when
submerged in water, so they should last as long as the
flowers. Small berries can be layered on top of one
another to create bands of color, and there are plenty of
vibrant varieties to choose from. This eye-catching
display places cranberries above gooseberries in a bowl
half full of water. Purplish-blue cornflower heads float
on top, forming a sumptuous contrast with the rich red
of the cranberries.

Hang on in there

Roses, a traditional favorite for so many of us,
look just as good in minimalist modern displays as
they do in old-fashioned bouquets. In this clever
arrangement, nine glowing orange blooms dangle their
straight stems into the water, suspended above a square
vase by a grid of sturdy grasses. Use raffia to tie together
the strands of grasses, then trim the ends neatly so that
they extend past the sides of the vase by at least 3/4
inch. Cut all the rose stems to the same length, slightly
shorter than the depth of the vase, and settle the
flower heads in the grid.

High style

Narcissus have a dreamy fragrance that will fill your home with the scent of spring. Make the most of them by gathering a big bunch together and anchoring them among sand and pebbles in a deep glass vase. Take a few flowers in one hand, with the stems parallel and the heads massed together. Keep adding more until you form a ball of blossoms. Tie the stems with ribbon or twine below the blooms, then cut the stems to the same length. Set them in the vase and surround with white sand and gravel. Fill up the vase with water.

TIP
Narcissus stems emit a slime that poisons other flowers, so if you want to use freshly cut blooms in a mixed display, first stand them in deep water containing a drop of bleach for 24 hours.

Heads together

When tulips are cheap and abundant in spring, buy a few
bunches of your favorite colors and use them to turn
square vases into bright building blocks. Using blooms
of all one shade in each vase, snip the stems short so
that the heads sit beneath the rim, in a shallow amount
of water. Include enough stems so that the flowers
support each other and remain upright. Fill a few vases
with identical arrangements and place them in an
orderly row, or even stack them on top of one another
for added impact.

TIP
Tulips are heavy drinkers,
so remember to top up
the vases frequently.
Unlike most flowers,
they prefer the water
to be cool rather than
lukewarm.

Sun worshippers

Sunflowers are the ultimate feelgood flower, their big cheerful faces glowing with the warmth of Midwestern summers. They are readily available as cut flowers, last for weeks and have an ebullient character that makes an impact without requiring clever arranging. This plastic vase in citrus yellow emphasizes the color of the flowers, its tone and texture adding a fresh, modern edge to their naive, rustic appeal. Arrange them casually, loosely grouping a few stems together, and cut them so that the large, heavy heads sit on the rim of the vase.

TIP
If a few sunflowers in your bunch have damaged petals, simply pull them off. The seedheads look striking on their own or in a display with other flowers.

Eastern promise

With oriental overtones, this stunning arrangement contrasts exotic pink peony heads with the dark metal of a galvanized planter, balancing the flowers on a grid of pretty colored bamboo. Fill the planter with water and cut bamboo skewers so that they extend about 1/2 inch beyond the sides of the planter. Tie the sticks together with twine to make a simple grid and place over the planter. Cut some peony heads, leaving enough stem to reach the water, then mass them in the center of the grid.

TIP
Plain bamboo skewers are easy to fid, and it's easy to paint them in the color of your choice.

Foam star

These peonies are arranged in a dark red loose-powder
form of florist's foam, which fills a clear glass vase and
picks up on the punchy pinks of the blooms. Although
today's fuss-free displays mean foam is not used as much
as it once was, the water-absorbent foam still comes in
handy for making stems stay exactly where you want
them. Traditionally available only in green or brown, it is
a secret that florists used to keep well hidden. But
nowadays comes in a range of fabulously bright colors
and looks good enough to be seen.

Simply red

Scarlet carnation heads bring a touch of floral fancy
to this tray of twinkling candles, as the frilly silhouettes
of the petals cast their reflections in the still water.
To create this sleek, contemporary display, choose
a square Japanese-style tray or dish and pair it with
white candles of the same shape. Fill the tray with a
small amount of water, then alternate five candles with
five carnation heads, floating the flowers on the water. If
possible, choose flowers of the same color as the tray for
maximum impact.

Under water

Many modern flower displays have as much going
on inside the vase as outside, and in this one all the
interest occurs beneath the water. Make a tower of color
by submerging hydrangea heads in a tall glass cylinder.
Fill the vase with crystal clear water, then take one
blossom at a time and slowly push it down to the
bottom, continuing to add more until the vase is about
three-quarters full. Pour off any excess water so that
the amount left just covers the top blossoms.

Seeing double

Create two arrangements in one by placing a smaller glass vase inside a large one. For even greater effect, combine different shapes, such as a round vase inside a square one. Fill the larger vase with about an inch of water, then place a few long leaves or grass stems inside it and fan them out around the curves. Fill a smaller or narrower vase with water, then place it inside the larger one and use it to contain a simple arrangement of flowers or foliage. The displays shown here feature white geraniums and red orchids.

Boxing clever

Roses look luxurious but can be expensive, so try experimenting with the cheaper short-stemmed varieties. This fashionable idea packs a crowd of orange blooms into a galvanized metal planter. Soak some florist's foam in water, then fit it into the base of the planter. Trim the stems of about 20 roses to the same length, so that the heads sit just above the lip of the planter. Push the stems into the foam, making sure the heads are level, and fill in the gaps beneath the flowers with moss.

TIP
Flowers are likely to last longer in an arrangement where the stems are cut short, as water can reach the heads more easily.

Strawberries and cream

A display that looks good enough to eat would make an eye-catching centerpiece for a table or sideboard. Bold amaryllis heads bring an extravagant flavor to any arrangement. Here they are massed together in the center of a glass dish to form a lush dome of scarlet, which is encircled by a contrasting border of cream-petalled anemones and spiky gerbera in a pale shade of peach. A charger plate placed underneath the dish adds a decorative finishing touch, the spotted pattern of its border echoing the circle of smaller blooms.

TIP
If you are using an arrangement as a table centerpiece, make sure it is low enough not to block your guests' view across the table or make conversation difficult.

Budding genius

Related to buttercups, ranunculus have big, beautiful heads packed with papery petals, which look good both as buds and once the flowers are fully opened. Available in many colors, from delicate pastels to vivid reds and oranges, they can claim a place in many different styles of arrangements. In this chic contemporary display, the frosted glass of the conical container is complemented by white ranunculus buds, arranged in a circle around a single yellow head. They nestle just beneath the rim of the vase on a bed of moraea, its sprays of tiny yellow and green flowers helping to support the heavy ranunculus heads.

Sing the blues

While clear glass vases create an unobtrusive showcase for the natural beauty of flowers and stems, colorful containers can add an extra dimension to a display. The secret is to make the color work with the flowers. Here, an understated bouquet of greenish-white anemones surrounded by a collar of furry stachys leaves gets a bold, modern treatment when arranged in a tall blue vase. The blue complements the soft gray leaves of the stachys, and their elegant shapes are echoed by the gentle curves of the container.

TIP
A few other types of gray-leaved foliage you could try include sage, artemisia and santolina.

Slick mix

Texture can be as important an ingredient as color when you are combining two or more types of flowers or other natural materials. An exciting mix can create a very individual display—here spiky asclepiads seed pods sit alongside small pompon-like heads of yellow wild camomile, topped with frilly-petalled fragrant white hyacinths. The wire bowl adds a further texture, giving the display its modern edge. Arrange the flowers in a glass or plastic bowl and place this inside the basket, or line the basket with plastic and fill it with pre-soaked florist's foam.

Cool chrysanthemums

Chrysanthemums assume a sophisticated character in a display that sticks to a limited palette of white and green. Its appeal is boosted by a mixture of textures: soft pennisetia grass and spiky nigella seed pods combined with rows of small green-centered chrysanthemums, all crowned by a dramatic shaggy-head spider variety. To create the raised effect, use pre-soaked florist's foam that extends beyond the top of the vase. Alternatively, place a second narrow container inside the vase to hold the central chrysanthemum and leaves, then build up the additional material in layers, arranging it in the space between the inner and outer containers.

Lazy days

Set the scene for an alfresco family lunch in summer
with pots of sunny yellow marigolds plucked straight
from the garden. Old tin cans make excellent informal
containers; here their corrugated metal complements
the rustic gray wood of the table, while forming a shiny
contrast with its rough texture. Clean out your old food
cans thoroughly, fill them with water, and then place a
few big, droopy marigold blooms in each one, with their
heads resting just above the rim. Add enough foliage
to fill in the gaps.

Nesting instinct

With velvety purple pansies and eggshells nestling among moss in a wire basket, this unusual display would make a good talking point, perhaps as an Easter table decoration. Carefully break the tops off a few eggshells, making sure that the body of the shell remains intact. Line a wire basket with freshly gathered moss, then nestle the shells on top and fill them with water. Cut a few pansy heads, leaving short stems, and arrange them with the stems inside the eggshells so that the water keeps the flowers fresh.

China collection

White china containers are a feature of traditional country kitchens, so raid your cabinets for pots, jars and vases and line them up along a shelf or mantelpiece to make a charming grouped display. Fill any pots with compost, then plant them with flowering annuals, and use the other containers to show off fresh spring flowers such as narcissus. Sticking to a limited color theme of yellow and white for the flowers will help to enhance the plain and simple appeal of the china.

Old and new

Add a hint of country charm to a contemporary
room setting with a display of flowers and foliage in
a traditional container. This tall yellow enamel pitcher
plays host to a casual arrangement of chrysanthemums
and dahlias in refreshing colors, which complement
the room's light, modern decor. Pay a visit to a yard sale
or flea market and you should find it easy to pick
up "vases" with character. Make sure that they are clean
and watertight before you use them for flowers, or find
a glass or plastic container (a tumbler is ideal) that fits
inside to hold the blooms.

Tall story

This elegant, tree-like display is a modern classic that
works well with any strong-stemmed flowers. Arrange
a mixture of agapanthus and nerines in your hand,
bringing the blossoms together to make a ball shape.
Tie the stems with string, just beneath the flowers. Pull
the stems together to make the trunk of the flower tree
and trim them all to the same length, then bind near
the base using waterproof tape. Put a pin holder in the
bowl and push the bound ends of the stems into it
so that they stand upright. Cover the pin holder with
stones and add water.

TIP
A pin holder is an
old-fashioned flower
arranging tool made of a
bunch of little metal
spikes on a baseplate.
See if your mom or
grandma has one tucked
away before you go out
to buy one.

Rich pickings

Mix flowers and foliage gathered from your garden for a simple country-style display. Make this bouquet using pink roses, white ranunculus, green alchemilla and other assorted foliage, or see what your beds and borders have to offer. Arrange the material loosely in your hand, building from the center and alternating flowers and foliage as you work. Keep the display loose and informal to add to that countryside feel. Secure the stems with garden string and cut them to match the height of the vase. For further country charm, place a few more blooms in an old milk jug beside the main vase.

TIP
Pick flowers from your garden in the early morning or late evening. Place them in water immediately, or the stems will form an air-lock that prevents them from drinking.

A bit rough

Choose chunky, organic vases to set a rustic tone. The rough textures and natural shades of stone or terracotta planters form a fascinating contrast with the pretty colors and delicate petals of hydrangeas and roses. Pack plenty of hydrangea heads tightly into a vase, with the stems cut down and hidden from view, and include a collar of leaves beneath the flowers to strengthen the look. Roses would be expensive to use in the same abundance, so try floating just a head or two in a rustic bowl with a layer of colored gravel at the bottom.

TIP
Porous stone or clay containers not designed specifically as vases may not be watertight, so place a glass or plastic container inside to hold the arrangement.

Pastel palette

There's nothing like strongly scented flowers for bringing the outside indoors, and fragrant hyacinths will add a whiff of spring to your rooms long before the weather warms up. Often grown indoors from bulbs, they are now also widely available as cut flowers, which last extremely well. They come in a broad selection of colors, including exquisitely muted pastels such as this pale pink. These hyacinths are massed with white parrot tulips in stone-colored pots to create a light, natural effect. If you can't find pots this color, try painting plain terracotta ones using sample quart cans of paint, and finish with matte varnish.

TIP
Buy cut hyacinths in tight green bud with the color barely showing. The stem will continue to grow in water and the head will triple in size as the flower bells open.

Harvest festival

This display celebrates the warm but mellow hues
of autumn, which is when hydrangea blooms deepen
in color to rich reds, purples or lilacs. Here, they
are complemented beautifully by rosy apples and red
skimmia. Huge hydrangea heads look dramatic as cut
flowers and, although they are a little expensive, just one
or two go a long way when massed with fruit or foliage.
Place a smaller column vase inside a large one and fill
the gap in between with crab apples. Fill the inner vase
with water, arrange the hydrangeas and skimmia, then
add a few apples pushed onto sticks.

TIP
**Hydrangeas are prone
to wilting. To help keep
them fresh, drape damp
cloths over the blooms for
a few hours after cutting.**

Hi-tech hedge

A collection of flowers that you might see growing
around any country field, such as dill flower and cowslip,
is given a modern twist when displayed in a designer-
style test tube vase. The test tubes are wired together so
that they can be adjusted to form different shapes and
curves. Cut the flower stems to different lengths to get
a random-looking variation in height, then place two or
three stems in each test tube. If you use tall, top-heavy
flowers, flex the row of test tubes into a zig-zag shape to
make it stable.

Meadow fresh

In this informal bouquet, the bold exuberance of a
pair of sunflowers is softened by the surrounding foliage
and grasses. The huge blooms sit low among the other
materials, framed by sprays of golden lime bupleurum
and cream-edged dogwood leaves, while feathery
grasses froth out at the base. The homey style of the
display is enhanced by the rough pottery vase with its
buttermilk glaze. Build up the bouquet in your hand,
starting with the sunflowers, then adding the bupleurum
and dogwood and finally the grasses. Cut the stems to
the same length, and bind with twine before placing
in the vase.

Enchanted forest

A fascinating mixture of textures gives this display its
unique charm. Left to themselves, a bunch of green
parrot tulips massed together in a purple glass bowl
would have asserted a mood of modern sophistication,
but a collar of rough tangled roots disturbs their cool
to add a touch of drama. Twining around the leaves and
stems, the roots create an almost sinister air, their woody
texture contrasting with the smooth curves and heavy
glass of the vase and the satiny petals of the flowers.

Out of the woods

Oak leaves and twigs give a woodland feel to red and pink blooms, while a plain white glass vase shows off the richness of their autumn colors. Flat pink sedum blossoms contrast with globe-shaped red dahlias and papery-petalled hydrangeas. The flowers are arranged in clusters, with all of one type together, to heighten the contrast between textures. The oak leaves form a collar beneath them, and more are interspersed between the flowers to set off their strong hues. Stark twigs poke wildly from among the blooms, breaking the neat, rounded shape of the display and reinforcing the woodland inspiration.

Exotic mood

In this simple but striking display, lush leaves
and grasses form a dark foil for vivid red bouvardia
flowers, evoking an exotic, jungle-like feel. A square
stone pot is lined with ligularia leaves, their glossy
surface contrasting with the rough texture of the stone.
Place a small glass or plastic container inside the lined
pot and fill it with water, then put in the heads of
bouvardia—a flower that should never be left out of
water. Finally, loop strands of bear grass over the top
to look like the handles of a basket, tucking the ends
in under the leaves.

Ruby and sapphire

The jewel-like hues of glossy red hypericum berries and spiky blue sea holly will warm up any room. To give the colors and textures their full impact, mass flowers or materials of one type together. Here the sea holly and berries are arranged in a compact hand-tied bouquet, with the holly in the center and the berries forming a border around it. Take a few stems in your hand, starting at the center, then add a few more at a time to build up the bouquet. Tie with twine, then place in a bowl lined with a layer of silvery-gray cineraria leaves, which highlight the colors.

TIP

As an alternative to hypericum you could use viburnum berries, which are a vibrant metallic shade of blue.

Grass sundae

Dip into the wide selection of grasses now available at florists and you should find plenty of suitable material to make a gorgeous display. Here they spill abundantly from the top of a tall wooden container in an arrangement that resembles a giant ice-cream sundae. The tiny white blossoms at the base are gypsophila, or baby's breath, while fat furry caterpillars of setaria grass rest just above it. A varied mixture of other grasses, from long and blade-like to soft and feathery, completes the recipe.

TIP
In a predominantly green arrangement of foliage or grasses, including a variety of different textures and shapes is the key to success.

Design detail

Flowers can help bring the decor of a room to life, so
choose displays that enhance the interior style you
want to create. In this classic bathroom setting, with
cream-painted walls and furniture, the frowsy pink
peonies and lime-green roses add a welcome splash of
color. Displayed in an old tin ewer, which is perched on
a wooden stool, they create a decorative feature for a
bare corner, with the angular lines of the ewer and stool
offsetting the curved legs and carved detail of the pretty
period-style washstand nearby.

Round it off

Achieving a distinctive shape is one of the hallmarks of successful floral design, especially if you want to create a more formal, traditional-style arrangement. A conical vase makes it easy to set roses in a dome shape, without the need to deal with florist's foam. Strip the leaves and thorns from 18 white roses, then place the outer circle of blooms in place, trimming the stems so that the heads sit against the edge of the vase. Add the next layer, trimming the stems so that the heads are raised just above the first ones. Continue adding layers until the vase is full.

TIP
Most roses available as cut flowers have no fragrance, so if you want scented ones look for the more expensive garden or old-fashioned varieties.

Purple prose

Valued for their delightful fragrance and range of colors, sweet peas evoke images of old-fashioned cottage gardens. They look best arranged on their own, without other foliage or flowers, and here a purple vase gives a modern edge to a big bunch of scented sweet peas in the same color. Be generous with the number of flowers, and gather them together to form a ball before cutting the stems to length. In this slender vase the stems are packed in tight, so as to retain the shape.

Global support

Flamboyant white lilies add instant glamour to a
room, as well as a rich perfume. They are also tougher
than they appear, lasting extremely well as cut flowers.
Their long stems give them a stately presence in
tall containers, but if you want a more compact
arrangement for a smaller room they can be equally
effective if cut down, so that the heads rest on the
lip of a round vase. The glossy white surface of this
vase works well as a contrast to the crazy heads of
Casablanca lilies, creating a cool, sophisticated look.

TIP
**If you get lily pollen on
your clothes, remove it by
taking a piece of Scotch
tape and patting it on the
dust. Don't rub, or the
pollen will stain.**

Big-headed beauties

A low, wide-necked vase such as this goldfish bowl is the best option for flowers with top-heavy heads, such as peonies. With their stems trimmed short so that their heads are supported by the rim of the vase, blooms in red, pink and white mass together in a glorious explosion of color. The stems are concealed by a large calathea leaf. First trim the stem of the leaf, then wrap it around your hand and release it inside the vase so that it unfurls close to the glass. Add water, then arrange the peonies, including a few leaves near the neck of the vase.

TIP
If you find it hard to make stems stay in place in a wide-necked vase, make a grid across the top using tape, leaving enough space to insert the stems.

Shaping up

A classic architectural arrangement gets a softer look with the use of puffball purple alliums and feathery asparagus fern. The decanter-style vase has a heavy base, which ensures that the tall display remains stable, while the narrow neck makes it easy to arrange the flowers. Trim the stems of five alliums to different heights, cutting the tallest about three times the height of the vase and the shortest so that the head rests on the rim. Add a few fern fronds to soften the outline.

TIP
Allium blooms have a faint onion odor that gets stronger as they age. Take care not to bruise the flowers when handling, as this will release even more of the smell.

Slimline

Snow-white peonies with extravagantly layered petals look twice as sumptuous when juxtaposed with the rich purple tint of this glass vase. The elliptical shape of the vase makes it perfect for narrow windowsills or mantelpieces, and the sturdy base enables it to support heavier displays safely. Cut the peonies so that the lowest heads sit just above the rim and the remaining ones just above these, and include plenty of leaves to provide some background color for the white flowers.

TIP
If you don't have a tinted vase, try adding a few drops of food dye to the water to get the color you want.

Vintage chic

A casual country-style gathering of summery garden flowers in glass bottles is given a refined air with the addition of a shiny silver tray. You can pick up vintage glass bottles inexpensively at yard sales and flea markets —look for ones with colored as well as clear glass, and collect a variety of sizes and shapes. Here blue and green bottles echo the colors of the flowers and foliage, which include blue muscari, white sweet peas, dill flower, blue nigella and a selection of grasses.

Perfectly plain

For a look of understated elegance that works well
in both period and contemporary homes, choose plain
containers with gently flowing curves. A white vase that
tapers towards the bottom is perfect for a dome-shaped
arrangement of pastel-colored roses, punctuated by
a few in a deeper pink. Cut the stems so that the lowest
heads sit just above the rim, with the others resting on
top of them. A few more heads nestling at the base of
a glass container add to the flower power, while the
mirror throws back reflections of the whole display.

The full works

A tall, conical vase has an elegant air by itself, and an exotic arrangement that brings together a tiger-stripe Singapore orchid and calathea leaves more than does it justice. But this display has even more visual excitement to offer, as the base of the vase is filled with iridescent, pearly oyster shells. Decorative pebbles or beads would also look good. This idea means you can get away with using shorter-stemmed, less expensive flowers in a tall vase, as the stems are concealed by the shells.

Twice as nice

You can't have too much of a good thing, so try splitting a bouquet of flowers between two identical containers to double its impact. The purple glass of these tall vases makes a perfect foil for cream-colored anemones, and complements the lilac tones of feathery sea lavender. Fresh green leaves add further color, and the delicate flowers and foliage are offset by the dark stems, visible through the glass. Group the anemones and leaves at the front of the arrangement, resting their heads on the vase rim, then use the sea lavender at the back to add height.

Light romance

Choose a palette of pale colors to complement a light, airy room. This feminine and fragrant bouquet features white lilac, creamy freesias and pink larkspur, all displayed in an elegant frosted vase. The waisted shape of the vase makes it easy to arrange the flowers. Cut the stems to varying heights to give some shape to the arrangement, but keep the overall look loose. Line up the freesias around the rim of the vase, with the sprays of lilac above them and the tall spires of larkspur fanning out at the back to add height.

Floating world

Some of the best modern arrangements can hardly
be called arrangements at all, as they require so very
little in the way of equipment, or even flowers! Invest
in a shallow glass bowl and you can create numerous
stunning displays simply by filling it half full with water
and floating blossoms and petals on top. Any blooms
that hold their shape in water will do. Roses are
perfect—in this bowl a large yellow bloom is surrounded
by a scattering of curling petals in scarlet and yellow.

Enduring relationship

If you want a display that will last longer than cut flowers, but are fed up with fussy, dust-gathering dried flower arrangements, this unusual idea may be more to your liking. For Zen-like simplicity in seconds, fill a tall, cylindrical glass vase about three-quarters full with hazelnuts, and then stand a single dried cotton branch among them. You don't even need water. If you can't find cotton branches, try experimenting with other natural dried matter, such as interesting seedheads or sculptural twigs.

Proud line-up

There's power in numbers, as they say, so to increase
the impact of a simple display, all you have to do is
repeat it a few times. Slender glass drinking tumblers
complement the graceful elegance of pink nerines,
whose flowers are a similar shape to lilies but on a
much smaller scale. The two nerines in each vase are
accompanied by curling stems of bear grass. A line-up
of three identical displays makes a chic decoration for
a narrow shelf or mantelpiece.

TIP
Nerines are readily
available in the winter,
so try combining them
with traditional Christmas
greenery to add an
exotic touch to festive
decorations.

What a dish

Pair it with a clever choice of containers, and all you
need is a single blossom to create a stylish display.
Think about the combination of colors and textures.
In a harmony of muted hues, the iridescent lilac tones
of this hydrangea head are offset beautifully by the soft
blue of the small bowl in which it sits. At the same time,
the delicate quality of its petals is enhanced by contrast
with the rough texture of the stone platter. Add a little
water to the small bowl to keep the flower fresh.

Poppy art

Flowers with colorful and flamboyant blooms are
more than capable of speaking for themselves, so they
are a great choice if you want an easy display that's
guaranteed to brighten up a room in minutes. Papery-
petalled Iceland poppies take a bow in a slender glass
vase, which is ideal for supporting their tall stems.
Simply cut them to different lengths so that each bloom
finds its own level. In a display with only a few flowers,
make sure they are all in good condition, with no bruised
or torn petals to spoil the effect.

TIP
Poppies can wilt quickly
as they lose a lot of sap
when cut. To prevent this,
seal the ends of the stems
by burning them with a
match or lighter.

Orient express

The Japanese are masters of simplicity when it comes to flowers and gardens, so take a leaf out of their book for a taste of oriental style. A tall, shapely vase and a few sprigs of fluffy white blossoms will put you on the right road in seconds. The tender green twigs are complemented by the dark olive tones of the crackleglaze vase, creating a look that combines a fresh springtime feel with an air of formal elegance. To emphasize the oriental tone, add a bamboo tray and a few pieces of white porcelain.

Sharp looks

Flowers or leaves that have distinctive shapes, such as this gloriously spiky sea holly, are ideal candidates for simple treatment. A tough character like this doesn't even need an elegant vase to catch the attention. Here a single stem has been slipped into an old glass bottle, which was picked up for just $1 at a market. You may well have similar containers lurking in your kitchen cabinets, such as old sauce bottles or jam jars. Of course, if they've held food, make sure you clean them out thoroughly first.

Bowl 'em over

This one's got it all—it's inexpensive, easy to do and simply gorgeous. A few sprays of flowers and greenery are all you need for this beautiful display that highlights the curves of a round glass bowl. Make sure the bowl is sparkling clean, then pour in about 2 inches of water. Cut the sprays to size so that they wrap loosely around half the bowl. Place some bear grass in first, then a long strand of variegated ivy, and finally one or two deep blue delphinium spikes, tucking all the cut ends into the water.

Cheerful outlook

With their brilliant colors and bold black centers, anemones resemble the sort of flowers that might appear in a child's painting, so they are a perfect choice if you want to brighten up a dull corner of a kitchen or family room. An informal display complements their cheery character; simply take a few clear glasses or bottles in varying sizes and slip a few stems into each, resting the blossoms on the rims of wide-necked tumblers. Group two or three glassfuls together.

TIP
Anemone flowers open in light and heat and close when it is dark and cool. They also incline their heads toward light, so bear these factors in mind when choosing a site for your display.

Bend me, shape me

Capture the carefree mood of spring with a few pretty
pink tulips and curved stems of budding willow, casually
intertwined within a glass vase. Pour a small amount
of water into the vase, then place three switches of
willow together and curl them around inside. Add three
tall tulips, their stems cut to a length of about 22 inches,
and gently fold each one into an arch shape, making sure
you place the stems in the water. As a finishing touch,
gently float a few fully open tulip heads on the surface
of the water.

Still waters

Conjure up an air of Zen-like calm with this super-quick
display idea for calla lilies. Plain as black and white,
yet big on contemporary chic, it uses four white lilies
laid horizontally across a square black dish to create an
oriental-style arrangement that's as simple as it is stylish.
Cut the lily stems to the right length, then fill the base of
a small curved dish with enough water to cover the ends
of the stems. Add a handful of shiny black pebbles to
hold them in place.

Petal power

This ultra-simple idea takes traditional red roses and uses them in a modern display that would make a perfect focal point for an empty fireplace. All you need to do is strip off the stems and scatter whole heads and petals around a large white candle in the base of a wide glass vase. This is an effective way of using the cheaper small-headed roses, which tend to look rather cheap in conventional arrangements. Add to the abundance of red by scattering more petals on the hearth around the base of the vase.

Single-minded

Some people find a whole bunch of sunflowers too
bright and garish. If you're among them, try sticking
a single stem into a sleek bottle vase for a much more
subtle option. The base of the glass vase is filled with
sand, in a rich terracotta shade that complements the
rustic tones of the sunflower. The sand serves to steady
the tall vase, while a large test tube embedded within it
holds water and supports the long stem of the flower.

Going solo

One exquisite white bloom, one beautiful vase—
bring them together for the perfect, elegant display.
The visual rewards far outweigh the tiny effort of
filling the vase about a third full with water and floating
a single blossom on top. The only skill comes in the
choice of vase and bloom; go for a flower with a large,
showy head, such as this white peony. Any shapely,
wide-necked, clear glass vase will do, but the white
band across the top of this one gives maximum effect
by seeming to enclose and frame the peony while
echoing its color.

TIP
The right time to buy
peonies is when the buds
are showing some color
and feel soft to the touch.
A bud that is too firm will
probably never open.

Bead necklace

It may seem like cheating, but a single flower in a simple glass vase or tumbler can make as strong a statement as an entire bouquet. If you want to show your friends that a little more creative thought has gone into the display, add a decorative touch by floating some brightly colored beads on the surface of the water. Here the red beads are an exact match for the color of the frilly carnation, creating an effect that's effortlessly elegant.

TIP
Cut carnation stems between the nodes—the thick, fibrous parts where buds or leaves emerge. This allows water to penetrate the stem more easily.

Trendsetters

One way to ensure that your flower displays are right up to date is to look for cutting-edge containers. There are new types of vases out there that make it simple to create designer-style looks. The curvaceous model at the back is almost entirely enclosed, with one opening at each end, while the vase in the foreground is a ball of glass punctuated with two openings. Invest in containers like these, then save money on flowers—all they need is a few distinctive blooms such as these burgundy dahlias. Stems of zig-zag asparagus fern add a softer touch.

TIP
Flowers of one type in a vase will last longer than a mix of different varieties, and a single bloom will survive longer than many blossoms of the same type.

Glass act

The beauty of a hand-tied bouquet is that it can be put straight into a vase for a simply stunning display. Encasing the entire thing in a tall square block vase gives a cool, contemporary twist to this cheery bunch of yellow tulips. Take about 20 stems and arrange them so that the heads are at different levels. Trim all the stems so that they are even on the bottom and tie the bouquet with raffia. To make a glass showcase, find a square vase that is tall and wide enough to take the full height of the tulips, and fill it with water to just below the first blossoms.

TIP
Always re-cut the stems of a bouquet you have been given before arranging the flowers in water. This opens up fresh fibers that take up the water more easily.

Summer nights

When the weather warms up and dining moves
outdoors, treat your guests to a candlelit feast
accompanied by a few of these enchanting table
decorations. Summer flowers and twinkling tealights
are sure to bring out the romance of balmy evenings
and, best of all, they can be assembled in minutes.
Place a simple glass tumbler on a saucer and pour a
small amount of water into both. Pick the heads off
a selection of summer flowers, and arrange them
with a few leaves in the saucer. Float a tealight on
the water in the glass.

Winter wonderland

Take a break from traditional reds and golds at Christmas and go for a cooler look with white roses, spiky purple sea holly, silver-painted twigs and a few sculptural seedheads. Bring it all together in a loose arrangement, adding plenty of dark green leaves and a few sprays of variegated ivy, then display in a plain white vase. The simple detailing around the top of this tall container adds a suggestion of snowflakes. For extra sparkle, pile a few silver and purple baubles in a white bowl and place it alongside the arrangement.

TIP
Paint dried material, such as twigs and pine cones, using spray paints. Work in a well-ventilated room and cover surrounding surfaces well.

Christmas classic

Make this formal candle centerpiece a focal point for
your Christmas table. Take a shallow circular glass dish
and cut pre-soaked florist's foam to fit, making it a little
narrower than the bowl's diameter, but 1/4 inch higher
taller. Tuck wide tropical green leaves down the sides,
then add more water. Insert three candles in the center
of the foam, using special candleholders available from
florists. Add pine, holly and poppy seedheads, letting
them trail over the edge. Group roses loosely into
groups of three, cut the stems to 6 inches and place
among the greenery. Tie ribbon bows onto wire and
insert at intervals.

To complement the
centerpiece, make ties for
plain white napkins using
a red rose attached with
wire to a twist of ivy.

Stalk talk

The stems make almost as much impact as the flowers when a clear glass vase is used to display this colorful handmade bouquet. Prepare red, orange and pink roses by removing the thorns and leaves. Lay the first stem in the palm of your hand and add more roses, turning the bunch as you go. Finally, add large waxy leaves so that they lie beneath the flowers. Secure the bouquet with twine, trim the stems so they're level on the bottom and place in a vase with a narrow neck, splaying out the stems from the base.

Best of the bunch

Hand-tied bouquets are an easy way of creating elegant arrangements, whether to decorate your own home or to wrap up and give as a gift. The most pleasing examples feature flowers and foliage in a range of textures and sizes, and this colorful bunch includes pink roses, cockscomb, flowering mint and dill. Lay the main blooms across the palm of your left hand, then set more flowers at a slight diagonal. Continue to build up the bouquet, rotating it in your hand until it is the size you want. Tie firmly with twine, then trim the stems so they're even at the bottom.

Instant sparkle

If you don't have time to make an elaborate decoration
for your Christmas table, dress it up in minutes with
a handful of blossoms and some sparkling sequins.
Fill a shallow glass bowl halfway with water, then cover
the base with glass beads and float a layer of sequins on
top. Snip off a few impressive blossoms, such as roses
and lilies, and float these in the water. Secure a few more
sequins to the petals with drops of water, then surround
the dish with tealights in small pearlized bowls.

Festive welcome

Dress your front door for Christmas with a wreath
that combines traditional berried ivy and snowberries
with more unusual blue thistles and lilac freesias.
Soak a florist's foam wreath frame in water, then cut 6-
inch stems of berried ivy and snowberries and stick
them into the foam until it is completely covered.
Intersperse with thistles and freesias, adding more until
the wreath looks full and balanced. Add a touch of
sparkle with embroidery stones, available from craft
shops, by gluing them onto the ivy leaves using a small
amount of clear all-purpose adhesive.

**Foam wreath frames are
cheap and are available
from florists and garden
centers. Follow the
manufacturer's soaking
instructions before
inserting the flowers
and foliage.**

Snow white

Narcissus are widely available at Christmas, and
this flower and candle combination makes a fresh,
modern alternative to traditional festive displays.
Place a large pillar candle in a flat-based glass bowl.
Make four bunches of flowers by gathering a few stems
in your hand, then adding more to form a ball
of blossoms. Tie with string, and cut the stems so
the flowers sit on the rim of the bowl. Wrap aspidistra
or laurel leaves around the stems of each bunch and
bind with golden wire. Place the "flower trees" around
the candle and fill the bowl with water.

Feminine touch

This pretty bouquet, full of enchanting pastel colors and spring fragrance, would make a delightful Mother's Day present. Group together parrot tulips, hyacinths and folded aspidistra leaves into a bouquet, starting from the center by holding a few blooms in your hand, then alternating the flowers and foliage as you build up the bouquet. Cut the stems to similar lengths and tie with string. Finish by wrapping fine tissue paper around the flowers—you'll need about three sheets—and secure with a pink or lilac ribbon tied in a bow.

TIP
Hyacinth stems secrete a poisonous liquid, so wear gloves when handling them or wash your hands immediately afterward.

Rosy posy

With their luxuriously multi-petalled heads, rich colors
and romantic associations, roses are the perfect choice
for a really special gift bouquet. If you want to treat
someone, take about 20 roses, remove any thorns and
leaves, and bundle them together into a bouquet,
twisting the stems and tying them in the middle with
a narrow ribbon. To add a bit of decoration, take a roll
of fine silver wire and make twisted knots at 4-inch
intervals. Wrap the wire gently around the head of the
bouquet and secure the ends among the stems.

TIP
Removing rose thorns is
necessary if you're making
a bouquet but it can
damage the stems, so ease
them off very carefully
using a sharp knife.

Heavenly scent

Put together this aromatic bouquet as a gift, or make it for yourself and display in a galvanized planter, which makes a steely contrast to the pastel blossoms. Take about 10 pink and white roses, plus variegated ivy and fragrant foliage such as eucalyptus and rosemary. Starting with a few flowers at the center, work outward, building up the bouquet in your hand to form a rounded shape. Secure the stems with string, then trim them all to the same length. Display in the planter so that the bouquet rests on the rim, with the outer blooms hiding its edge.

Funtime

Formal bouquets are fine for special occasions, but if you simply want to cheer someone up you can't beat a casual collection of cottage-garden favorites. Have fun with bold hues, choosing a bold color combination such as sky-blue delphiniums and orange snapdragons. Bring them together to make an informal bouquet by taking a few stems in your hand and adding a few more at a time, finally encircling the flowers with hosta leaves at the base. Tie with brightly colored twine and trim all the stems to the same length.

TIP
If you want to make a smaller arrangement, you could swap the delphiniums for blue cornflowers or lilac Chinese asters.

In the can

Get into the habit of saving old food cans and you'll
have a constant supply of quirky containers just waiting
for the right flowers to come along. Where would you
find a more appropriate holder for an exuberant bunch
of summer sunflowers than an old sunflower oil can?
This one has an illustration to provide a double helping
of blooms and a green background that's a perfect
match for the leaves. Use a can opener to remove the
top, then clean the can thoroughly before filling with
water. Look out for sharp edges left by the opener
when handling.

CONSUMER'S
PRIDE
GUARANTEED
PURE
SUNFLOWER
OIL
Solsikkeolje
PRIDE OIL PRODUCTS
PRIDE HOUSE, WEMBLEY STADIUM INDUSTRIAL ESTATE,
SOUTH WAY, WEMBLEY, MIDDLESEX. HA9 0HB.
TELEPHONE 0181-900-0736 FAX 0181-900-1417

Squash game

Filled with fiery Chinese lanterns to light up a room, a hollowed-out butternut squash makes an original natural container. Slice a sliver off the bottom of the squash to create a flat base and make it stand, then cut off the top and scoop out enough of the vegetable to hold and hide a small vase. Put some water in the vase and arrange the stems of Chinese lantern. Any other large fruits or vegetables that have firm skins could also lead a double life as vases—try watermelons or pumpkins, for example.

TIP
If your vegetable vase seems a little wobbly, stick a few pieces of poster putty to the base to help it stand firm.

Bright beakers

A search through your kitchen cabinets can often
turn up some cool containers. Floral flair relies on dash
rather than cash, and a successful marriage of flowers
and vases is more important than the elegance of one
or the other. Even humble plastic cups can shine when
teamed up with the right flowers. These in brilliant green
and blue complement perfectly the hot pinks and
purples of anemones. Cut the flower stems so that the
heads rest on the rim of the cup. Place a few of these
colorful arrangements side by side to brighten up a
shelf or windowsill.

Net results

There's no need to limit your search for original containers to those that can hold water. This mesh bag looks interesting, while the purple hyacinths and anemones get their drink from a tall glass hidden inside. To make the bouquet, take six hyacinths and 18 anemones. Hold a couple of stems in your hand, then add more so that they form a spiral. When the bouquet is complete, secure the stems with a rubber band, then trim them all to the same length. Place the flowers inside the glass, fill it with water, and slip the glass into the bag.

Rescue mission

A windy day in the garden can leave some blooms broken off. Don't let them go to waste—pick them quickly and arrange in an assortment of glass bottles in different sizes and shapes, the more traditional the better. Here pink veronica, deep red snapdragon, white allium, dusty pink helleborus and a purple sweet pea all go into the mix, and are shown off in jam jars and old drink bottles made from clear and green glass. If you can't find suitable glassware at home, see what you can pick up at markets or garage sales.

Metal magic

If you have trouble arranging flowers in wide-necked vases, these easy-to-make metal covers could help. Create a template by drawing around the rim of your vase on paper, then draw out from this to design to add the sides of the cover. Cut out the template and use it to cut the same shape from thin metal. Mark around the edges with a pen, then cut out the design with small, sharp scissors. Using a hole punch, make evenly spaced holes for flowers in the top part of the cover and decorate the side edges with tiny holes. Place over the vase and fold down the edges.

Get the wrap

If you're bored with your old vases or they look too fussy for contemporary floral designs, give them an instant update with a wrapping of fresh white fabric. Take any upright vase and loosely swathe it with a fine white material, such as muslin or voile. Be generous with the amount of fabric to create a flamboyant look and thoroughly conceal the vase. Secure by binding it with wire or cord. Choose matching white flowers for a sophisticated display—here tulips and ranunculus are teamed with lysimachia and silver-painted ting ting.

TIP
For a more sumptuous look, wrap your vase in richly colored silk. Fill it with bold blooms, such as roses or peonies, in strong coordinating shades.

Take the tube

Test tubes are just the right size and shape to hold a single flower stem, and are also cheap to buy. Get a collection of them and use lengths of ribbon or raffia to suspend them from a shelf, curtain rod or window frame. Tie the ribbon or raffia securely around each tube and attach it to the underside of a shelf or frame with push pins. Use a pitcher to partially fill the tubes with water, then slip in the blooms. Flowers with fine stems, such as roses, sweet peas or freesias, are the most suitable.

TIP
You could use this idea to decorate your Christmas tree. Hang the tubes from the branches using gold or silver wire or shiny ribbon instead of raffia.

Triple treat

Team shiny tin cans with stately delphinium spikes and line them up on a mantelpiece or along a dinner table to make a dramatic modern display. Save three identical food cans, then clean them out and soak off the labels. Cut blocks of florist's foam to fit in the cans, leaving space at the top for pebbles, then soak the foam in water before placing inside. Cut three delphinium stems the same length and insert into the foam. Conceal the foam with a layer of white pebbles.

TIP
If possible, choose cans with ring-pull lids. These won't have the sharp, jagged edges left by a can opener.

Pretty in pink

Matching your vases to the color of the flowers creates a powerful impression, and dressing them up in fabric makes it easy to achieve that coordinated look. Stiff gauze wrapped around clear glass tubes echoes the delicate pink of these tulip heads. Sheer enough to diffuse the light, it also allows a glimpse of the long, graceful stems. Cut a piece of fabric large enough to wrap around the vase, allowing for a small overlap, then secure neatly with clear glue. For maximum impact, group a few tubes together, with a single tulip stem, complete with leaf, in each.

TIP
Tulips will bend their heads toward the light so turn the vase daily to keep them straight.

Tangerine dream

The graduated orange effect on these glass vases
may look as though it has come straight out of a
designer's studio, but anyone can achieve it using
a can of spray paint. Work in a well-ventilated area and
cover surrounding surfaces with newspaper. It's a good
idea to spray the vase inside a large, open cardboard
box to avoid too much mess. Choose a vase with a
smooth surface and apply light coats until you are
satisfied with the effect. For a graduated look, direct the
spray at the point where you want the densest color—
around the rim or base.

Bags of tricks

Glassware and china shops are the obvious places to search for containers, but look elsewhere and you may come home with some interesting finds. Have you tried your local candle store, for example? There are lots of pretty paper and fabric votive candleholders around, which make great little vases. These mesh bags have a glass inside intended to hold the candle, but it's also just the right size to accommodate a single flower with a big bright head, such as a carnation. Repetition increases the impact, so place a row of at least six down the center of a dining table or along a mantelpiece.

Putting on the glitz

Pop one or two flamboyant blossoms into a sequined
handbag to make a sparkling display that would be
perfect for adding some glamour a bedroom.
Hydrangeas have the panache to carry off this quirky
idea, and with the delicate lilac petals picking up on the
color of the bag, flowers and container look as if they
were made for one another. To hold and nourish the
blooms, place a drinking glass or empty jam jar inside
the bag and add water, or make a waterproof lining
using a plastic bag and fill it with pre-soaked florist's
foam.

Veggie showstopper

Ornamental cabbages have the looks to lift them out of
the vegetable patch and into a starring role as potted
plants. With a collar of frilly leaves cradling a bright pink
center, they are sure to capture the attention, and will
add a touch of drama to any room. For a hint of potting-
shed ruggedness, wrap their pots in plastic and then
cover this with jute or burlap. Wrap a length of it around
the pots a few times, then tie with raffia.

Feeling hot

Bring a dash of spice into your home with red-hot chili peppers and solanum, whose berries resemble small tomatoes. Plant them in square or round galvanized metal cans for a gritty city flavor. Grown for their decorative fruits, ornamental peppers, are usually sold at Christmas, although summer-flowering types are also available. The fruits darken with age from yellow to orange before they finally turn red. Solanum plants are also popular during the festive season, and their round fruit turns from green to orange-red.

Leaf dressing

When there's still a winter chill outside, it's such a delight
to see potted bulbs coming to life indoors and opening
their buds to proclaim the start of spring. Daffodils and
narcissus can be planted indoors or out, although they
last longer outside. Plant the bulbs in autumn, to flower
the following spring. If your regular houseplants have
laid claim to all your pretty pots, pick up a few large
waxy leaves from your local florist and use these to
conceal unattractive plastic containers. Stick one end to
the pot with Scotch tape, then wrap the leaf around and
tie with raffia.

TIP
If you find it difficult to
keep the leaf in place,
stick it to the pot more
securely using a little
double-sided tape.

Goldfish bowl garden

Make a decorative planter for succulents using a goldfish bowl. Put a line of masking tape around the inside, about a third of the way up, and paint the inside surface of the bowl green below this line using household oil-based paint. Continue the paint over the lower edge of the tape to make sure you get a clean line. When the paint is dry, remove the masking tape and fill the bowl up to this line with plant compost. Plant an aloe vera flanked by a couple of small cacti, then scatter colored mosaic or broken tiles over the surface of the compost.

Clear winners

Sculptural plants such as succulents suit modern interiors well, so give them chic containers to match. Browse around the houseware stores and you'll find it easy to pick up some original ideas; these clear acrylic containers are intended for storing stationery, yet they do a perfect job as planters. Fill them with white gravel that you press along the walls, leaving a hollow in the middle. Then bury the roots and soil of the succulents in the hollow, so that they're not visible. Cacti and succulents should be watered frequently between spring and autumn, but only sparingly in winter.

TIP
Rather than burying the roots and soil in the gravel, you may find it easier to leave the plants in their original pots and simply conceal these among the stones.

Go-anywhere plant

With their beautiful flowers on tall stems, potted lilies
are extremely versatile. They look elegant in understated
classic interiors or minimalist modern rooms, but are
also striking enough to hold their own among brilliant
colors and modern decor. This fragrant pot variety,
Lilium oriental, has flowers splashed with pink that echo
the vibrant shade on the wall behind, while the lime
green pot provides a bold contrast. Lily pollen
can stain clothes and carpets, so you may want to
remove the stamens—do this by pulling them off with
your fingers. Water the plant moderately and feed
lightly once a week.

TIP
**When they have finished
flowering, potted lilies
can be planted out in the
garden in a semi-shaded
spot. They will flower
again the following year.**

'70s revival

Firm favorites in 1970s homes, spider plants later fell out of fashion. But now these easy-to-grow plants are being appreciated for their retro appeal. Give them an instant update by displaying them in brightly colored rattan pots. Place in a bright, sunny spot, then keep them supplied with lots of water and a weekly feed, and they will reward you with the familiar cascade of fine leaves. In addition, the flowering stems produce miniature plants, which can easily be removed and propagated to make new ones. The club-like roots should be repotted every year.

TIP
Spider plants can rid an enclosed space of carbon monoxide, so use them to combat traffic fumes by lining up a few pots along a windowsill.

Flame effect

Add a flicker of warmth to a pale, neutral color
scheme with the brilliant flame-like flowers of this
showy bromeliad. Vrieseas are native to Central and
South America, so this striped, ethnic-inspired pot
makes a fitting container, reflecting the plant's origins
and balancing the bright colors of its leaves and flowers.
In the wild, vrieseas are adaptable plants, thriving in
both damp forests and cooler, dry regions, but indoors
they do best in a warm, humid atmosphere. The roots
should be kept moist but not wet; if possible, use water
that has been boiled and then allowed to cool to a
lukewarm temperature.

Stripe tease

Pick up on the trend for stripes in home decor with
a neoregelia plant. Some varieties, like this one, have
variegated stripes running the length of their leaves.
Another striking asset is the pink or red color of
the rosette of leaves at the center, which also has tiny
flowers hidden inside. These bromeliads come from
the Amazon region and like temperatures of around
68°F and a bright spot, although not direct sunlight.
Water moderately into the rosette as well as the
compost, feed once a month and mist the leaves
regularly with a spray bottle.

Blending in

Delicate plants with classic looks, such as this pretty potted rose, can be made to look perfectly at home in a modern setting if they're displayed in the right containers. Try simple transparent holders made from clear glass or plastic, concealing the roots and compost among a soft bed of spongy moss. Potted roses flower well in a bright spot, as long as they are kept moist and fed once a week. To encourage regrowth, cut the plant back to 2 inches above the soil after it has finished flowering, and two months later you should see new flowers.

Shine on

An attractive plant can be a welcome addition to a home office, adding a natural touch among all the hi-tech equipment. The smooth, mirror-like surface of a shiny metallic pot heightens that textural contrast, offsetting the ribbed leaves and spiky orange flowers of this *Calathea crocata*. One of the few calatheas that produce flowers, its leaves have bronze-maroon undersides and close up at night. Place it in a bright spot but not full sun, in a temperature of around 68°F. Spray regularly and water sparingly.

TIP
Using hard water will cause water marks to appear on the leaves of calathea plants, so give them boiled water that has been allowed to cool.

Peace offering

Tall and serene, with shapely white flowers and long
shiny leaves, the peace lily will make its presence felt
in any room, and is more than capable of standing out
against a brightly painted backdrop. To make the most
of its height, plant it in a tall pot; the chic style and sharp
color of this planter is ideal for a bold, modern setting.
Peace lilies need a lot of water and should also be
sprayed occasionally, avoiding the flowers. Feed them
every other week. If you remove dead flowers regularly,
new ones should appear after four to six weeks.

TIP
**Many plants suffer from
dry air in centrally heated
rooms, so misting the
leaves, if recommended,
is an important part of
their care. Placing pots
in groups also helps to
increase humidity levels.**

PRACTICAL ADVICE

Steps to success

Today's trends in floral design play right into the hands of those of us too busy to fuss over formal arrangements. Simple and natural are the keywords, and as the displays in this book prove, you don't have to spend hours working with shape, form and color to produce spectacular looks. However, a few minutes devoted to preparing flowers and containers will keep your handiwork fresh and healthy for as long as possible.

Seeing that flowers never get thirsty and giving some thought to where you place your display will also extend their life. The following tips will help you give cut flowers the care they appreciate, so that they reward you with long-lasting looks. Individual varieties may have additional care requirements, so ask your florist for advice if you want to get the best from your blooms.

Buying fresh flowers

• To be sure of getting good-quality, long-lasting flowers, buy them from a reputable professional florist. Look for firm petals and healthy green leaves. Most flowers should be bought when they are in bud or half open, and buds should show a reasonable amount of color. Ones that are too tight may never open.

• Bouquets should be well wrapped to protect the flowers. If it will be several hours before you can put them in water, ask the florist to cover the ends of the stems with damp paper. Flowers can also be "aqua packed," with a tube of water around the stems.

• Check that cut flower food is

included with your blooms, and ask for some if it isn't. It usually comes in powder form, in a small plastic packet, but is also available as a liquid.

Conditioning your bought blossoms

• Don't rush to arrange your flowers as soon as you get them home. A little time spent preparing them, known as conditioning, will help extend their lifespan.

• Remove all the lower leaves and cut each stem at an angle about half an inch from its end. As soon as you have done this, place them in a bucket of deep, tepid water for six to eight hours to give them a good drink. (Generally cut flowers prefer tepid water, with the exception of spring flowers. These should always be conditioned with cold water.)

• If stems are bent, you can straighten them by tightly wrapping the whole bunch in brown paper and securing it with Scotch tape before placing the flowers in the water.

Flowers from your garden

• The best time to pick flowers is in the early morning or late evening, when the sun is low, the air is cool and the stems hold more water. Flowers cut in the heat of the day may wilt more quickly.

• Use garden shears or sharp scissors, and cut thicker stems or thin branches at an angle.

• Place the flowers and foliage in water immediately after cutting, otherwise air locks can form in the stems, reducing their ability to take in water. If necessary, carry a bucket outdoors with you, filled with tepid water that comes up to the flowers' necks. Leave them in the bucket for up to 12 hours before arranging.

Preparing containers

• Make sure vases are thoroughly cleaned before each use, as any lingering bacteria will harm fresh flowers.

• If you are using an unusual container, check that it is watertight. If not, line it with a jar or tumbler. (Some metals, such as zinc, can be toxic to flowers so it's best to line all metal containers just in case.)

• Choose a container that will be able to hold enough water to feed the number of flowers you are using.

• Fill your chosen container with lukewarm water, unless you are arranging spring bulb flowers such as daffodils or tulips, which prefer it cold.

• Sprinkle in the cut flower food supplied by the florist, which is designed to nourish the flowers, help them last and prevent bacteria build-up. Use the correct amount for your size of container. Don't be tempted to try suggestions for homemade flower foods, as these do more harm than good.

Arranging flowers

• To keep the water in the vase clean, make sure any leaves below water level have been stripped off, as rotting greenery will encourage harmful bacteria. When you are cutting the stems to the right length, snip diagonally to give them a larger surface area for absorbing water.

• Florist's foam is useful if you are creating a more formal arrangement with a distinctive shape, and want to make sure each flower keeps its position.

The dense foam comes in blocks that can be cut to fit your container, and it is able to absorb a significant amount of water to keep the flowers fresh. Soak it before arranging them, following the manufacturer's instructions.

• Another, simpler way of keeping flowers in place is to put scrunched-up chicken wire inside the vase.

Perfect positioning

• Flowers are used to being outdoors, so keep your display in a cool place, away from direct sunlight and hot radiators. Tight buds need sufficient light to open, but once they have done so, move them to a less bright position.

• Keep your flowers away from bowls of fruit. Ripening fruit emits a small amount of ethylene gas which causes cut flowers to age prematurely. Dying flowers have the same effect on fresh displays.

• Never place a vase of flowers directly on top of electrical equipment or polished furniture in case of unexpected leaks.

Looks that last

• To ensure that your flowers last as long as possible, top up the water (with food added) whenever necessary. Some flowers will make the water murky within a few days. If this happens, empty and rinse out the vase and refill it.

• Pinch off dead flowers and leaves to encourage other blooms to open and to prolong the life of your arrangement.

• Vase life varies for different flowers, so ask your florist's advice if you want to create a display that will be at its peak for a special occasion.

WHERE TO BUY:

FLORISTS IN YOUR AREA

BLOOMEN DIRECT FLOWERS AND GIFTS
Online directory of member florists in Canada and USA.
www.bloomendirect.com

CANADA FLORISTS DIRECTORY
Canada's largest directory of florists. Provides listings of more than 4,200 florists, shops and businesses.
www.canadasflorists.com

LOCATE-A-FLOWER-SHOP.COM
Nationwide directory of florists. Includes telephone numbers and delivery information.
www.locateaflowershop.com

THE FLOWER SHOP NETWORK
Verifies all local florists in their directory, and provides links to the FTC and MSNBC.
www.flowershopnetwork.com

FLORIST-NETWORK.COM
Specializes in finding best florist and most affordable price.
www.florist-network.com

AFLORAL.COM

Floral decorating company offering range of accessories and materials.
Tel:(888) 299-4100
afloral@alltel.net
www.afloral.com

BURLAP CREATIONS

Floral supplies and home décor store offering extensive range of natural and artificial accessories.
www.burlapcreations.com

COUNTRY HOUSE FLORAL

All the mechanics and accessories required to create floral designs.
Tel: (508) 255-6664
cohoflo@comcast.net
www.countryhousefloral.com

BEVERLY'S CRAFTS AND FABRICS

Save-on-Crafts.com and Floral Home Company
Offers discount savings on floral decorating materials.
Customer service
(831) 475-2954
or (831) 475-1801
help@beverly's.com
www.save-on-crafts.com

DRIED FLOWERS "R" US

Wholesale company that also sells direct to retail customers. Specializes in shipping dried and preserved flowers, mosses, grasses, wreaths and more.
Tel: (407) 740-0487
or toll free: 1-888-Larkspur

FLOWER DEPOT STORE

Offers changing selection of dried and preserved floral decorating products.
Toll free: 1-877-780-2099
dryflowrc@aol.com
www.flowerdepotstore.com

HAZEN & ASSOCIATES

Extensive range of mosses and baskets. Also stocks foams, hotwire cutters, hydrosorb and more.
Tel: (602) 978-1156
info@mossfoam.com
www.mossfoam.com

WATER-GEL CRYSTALS

Online suppliers of water-gel polymers. Ideal for making decorations with live plants, which can survive for weeks without being watered. For use in any shape, size, glass or plastic container.
info@watergelcrystals.com
www.watergelcrystals.com

FLORAL SUPPLIES

FRESH FLOWER WAREHOUSES

FLOWER OUTLET.COM

A Bay Area (CA) bulk-buyer of high quality flowers, stocked and re-stocked daily. Offers discounted prices closest to wholesale and overnight delivery.
www.floweroutlet.com
info@floweroutlet.com
Tel: (510) 450-1350

SPECIALIST SERVICES AND SUPPLIERS

WEDDINGFLOWERIDEAS.COM
Provides wedding flower planner, styling ideas, seasonal, allergy, and budgeting advice.
Tel:(205) 444-0769
barb@weddingflowerideas.com
www.weddingflowerideas.com

VINCENZA FLOWERS
Service offering full preservation of bouquets and floral arrangements. Provides shipping instructions.
Tel toll free: 1-888-CAN LAST
or 1-888-226-5278
www.syracuseweddings.com

LITTLE RED ROBIN
Offers child-sized gardening tools and flower arranging materials for young children.
Tel: (815) 777-0836
customerservice@littleredrobin.com

CONTAINERS AND ACCESSORIES

CRATE AND BARREL
Offers modern range of vases,
baskets and assorted containers.
Tel: 1-800-967-6696
24 hours a day
www.crateandbarrel.com

BED, BATH AND BEYOND
Stocks a wide variety of
accessories suitable for
flower arranging.
Toll free: 1-800 GO BEYOND
or 1-800-462-3966
24 hours a day
www.bedbathandbeyond.com

IKEA
International home furnishing
store offering funky, low-price
accessories, vases, baskets and
more.
www.ikea.usa.com
www.ikea.ca

DICK BLICK

Retail chain for art material and craft supplies.
Customer service
Tel: 1-800-723-2787
info@dickblick.com
www.dickblick.com

MICHAELS STORES

Range of floral and home décor products and craft materials.
Tel: 1-800-642-4235
www.michaels.com

CRAFTS

HIA Retail Outlets
Directory of on-line retail or mail-order craft businesses.
Search by US zip codes within five mile radius.
www.i-craft.com

SOCIETIES

SOCIETY OF AMERICAN FLORISTS

Floral education site with tips, flower-care advice, library and more.

www.aboutflowers.com

AIFD AMERICAN INSTITUTE OF FLORAL DESIGNERS

Non-profit organization established to promote the art of floral design.

Tel: (410) 752-3318

AIFD@assnhqtrs.com

www.aifd.org

CONTRIBUTORS

BBC Worldwide and *BBC Good Homes* magazine would like to thank the following contributors.

Marcus Crane Flowers: pages 33, 35, 89, 93, 133 Green: pages 103, 105, 135, 161, 163, 187, 189 Jane Hughes (at Rockett): pages 9, 11, 13, 15, 17, 47, 49, 55, 79, 81, 83, 107, 109, 111, 113, 115, 117, 145 165, 167, 169,173

Jane Packer: pages 19, 21, 23, 25, 27, 29, 31, 61, 63, 87, 121, 123, 127, 129, 131, 151, 153, 155, 179, 183, 185 Kate Kenyan (Plants &Flowers Association): pages 37, 39, 41,43, 45, 67, 69, 71, 73, 75, 77, 99, 101, 159, 197, 199, 201, 203, 205, 207, 209